AF438017

Frugal Living for Happiness & Freedom

Gideon Crusader

Published by Gideon Crusader, 2022.

While every precaution has been taken in the preparation of this book, the publisher assumes no responsibility for errors or omissions, or for damages resulting from the use of the information contained herein.

FRUGAL LIVING FOR HAPPINESS & FREEDOM

First edition. November 19, 2022.

Copyright © 2022 Gideon Crusader.

ISBN: 979-8201100766

Written by Gideon Crusader.

Also by Gideon Crusader

Magic Quest
A Codex on Creating a Magical Phantom
Prosperity Magic for Money & Wealth
Telekinesis Bible
Beware of the Modern World

Standalone
Frugal Living for Happiness & Freedom

Table of Contents

For MJ and all those who are seeking peace of mind, happiness, and freedom in this modern world...

Introduction

Frugal Living for Happiness & Freedom is a life manual that will teach you the importance of being frugal, as well as how you can live a happy and fulfilling life while spending very little money. No matter what people may tell you, the truth is that you do not need so much money in your life to be truly happy. In fact, many times, money is what misdirects us and blinds us from the real source of happiness in our life.

It should be noted that being frugal is not about being cheap. There is a big difference between being frugal and being cheap. You are not cheap. It is just that, when you are frugal, it only shows that you now understand and view money as it really is. It means that you now understand the real worth and value of money — and that now you know that you are not dependent on money for your happiness.

Frugal Living for Happiness & Freedom will give you the right foundation that you need to experience real happiness and freedom by living a frugal life. When you pursue this lifestyle, it is important that you have the right foundation. This foundation is based on your understanding and view as to what living a frugal life really means. In this regard, it is important that you have the right view on what money is really all about. In this book, we will discuss the importance of money and how it relates to happiness and the way of a frugal lifestyle.

Frugal Living for Happiness & Freedom reveals teachings that you can apply into your daily life right now at this very moment.

These teachings can create positive changes in your life. But, it is up to you to put the teachings into actual practice and actually make them work in your life. The good news is that it is actually easy to live a frugal lifestyle, and it will also help you achieve true happiness and freedom.

Are you ready to enjoy a frugal lifestyle? Are you ready to have more time in your hands and be happier in your life? If yes, then let me now welcome you into this beautiful world where love, peace of mind, and happiness are more important and valuable than money. This is the way of the true human being. Now is the time for you to actually live your life to the fullest and be who you truly are. Be happy and be free.

What is Frugal Living?

Frugal living is the kind of lifestyle where you do not depend on money to be happy. These days, so many people think that happiness is the answer to all of their problems. However, this is simply not true. In fact, it is simply an illusion that the world wants you to believe so that you will get stuck in its system. In fact, there are many rich people in the world who are very unhappy and unsatisfied with their lives.

It is sad to think that you would spend years earning money only to realize in the end that you have been chasing the wrong thing. If you give frugal living a chance, you might realize very important lessons in life much faster, and hopefully save you from a sad and regretful life.

It should be clarified that frugal living is not about being cheap. There is a big difference between frugal living and being cheap. You are not cheap. Cheap has a negative connotation and usually demonstrates bad taste or a low standard. When you are frugal, you do not sacrifice your decency. However, this time, you simply have a much healthier relationship with money. And, this time, you know that you do not need money (or at least not so much money) to be happy. In fact, when you are frugal, it even shows a more delicate taste since money is no longer the source of your happiness. Isn't it cheap and sad to think that someone's source of happiness is only money? Where is the soul in that?

Being frugal is a way of life that is different from the mainstream illusions of the world. Nevertheless, it is something that will allow you to be more alive and finally live your life with meaning instead of being continuously enslaved by the desire to earn money. Indeed, life should mean so much more than earning money.

It should also be clarified that being frugal does not mean that you are against money. Even if you are frugal, you will still be making use of money. However, this time, your relationship with money and how you view it will be much different. This time, you will see money as it really is, free from the many illusions of the modern world.

Living frugally is more like that fruit or effect of a certain realization than a mere means to an end. Becoming frugal is usually when you realize what you really need to be happy, as well as having a better view or relationship with money. As you can see, it is actually a path of self-discovery. Once you have this realization, then living frugally will naturally happen on its own.

Quick Review

- What is frugal living all about?

- Is being frugal the same as being cheap?

- Is it difficult to start living frugally?

What is Money to You?

How important is money to you? Does your personal happiness depend on money? If your happiness is primarily dependent on money, then chances are that your happiness is also an illusion. Long ago, people were happy without any money. Do not forget that money is a man-made creation. It is not a naturally-existing thing in the world. However, today, many people treat money in a very special way and hold it with much importance. Sadly, the are times when people view money as something more important than kindness, love, or even more valuable than human lives. Of course, this is a corrupt and wrong approach, and you must not follow this line of thinking.

Indeed, it is true that money can be helpful. Even people who are frugal are not against money. However, this time, we just know the real value of money, and that money has its inherent limitations.

It should also be noted that as long as you are exposed to this world, especially to this modern world, then money will always have its worth. However, this does not mean that everything is dependent on it. The truth is that we do not really need a huge amount of money to live a happy life. If you live a life that does not depend on money for happiness, then you might be surprised just how little money you actually need.

Money is not completely bad. In fact, even those who live frugally like money, but we are just not obsessed with it. So now, we have a much healthier relationship with it. We use money for our own benefits instead of letting money use us and control our lives.

Stop for a moment and think about the role of money in your life. Just how important is money to you? Is your personal happiness dependent on money? There is no wrong way of answering the said questions. The important thing is simply to be very open and honest with yourself.

The world has placed so much importance on money that so many people believe it. However, money is not the key to happiness. And, although money may buy the things that can make you happy, such kind of happiness is transient and even illusory. This is why we do not depend on money for happiness. In fact, one of the tests to know if a certain thing would lead to true happiness is to ask yourself if it is primarily based on money. If the answer is in the affirmative, then chances are that it would not lead you to true happiness.

Quick Review

- How important is money to you?

- Is your happiness dependent on money?

- What is a good test to ask yourself to know if something would lead to true happiness?

Money in the Modern World

In our world, money is given a very high importance. Many people also measure others by the amount of money that they make instead of the love that they give. It is up to you which way you view people — is it their money or their character?

The problem with having so much devotion to money is that it tends to defeat the real value of humanity. We must realize that we do but need to keep on following all the mainstream crap that is going on around us. We can make the decision to not limit ourselves to money by going well above it. This way, we can be free from all the constraints of money, as well as from all limitations that it brings.

Just because everyone around you is so obsessed with money does not mean that you should do the same. You always have a choice.

It is true that the lifeblood of our society is money. Money keeps everything going. However, if we limit ourselves to money, we will not be truly happy. Therefore, it is important to build a healthy relationship with money. We must know clearly the role of money in our lives and where we stand. Money may temporarily give pleasure to our material desires, but it can never truly satisfy the desires of the soul.

We live in a world where people directly and indirectly worship money. Just because we do not literally pray to money does not mean that we are not worshiping it. Worship can be demonstrated through other things than by praying, such as through our actions. For example, a person may steal just to satisfy his love for money. If we really want to have goodness and peace in our hearts, we cannot allow money to control us.

Money is not completely evil. However, we should learn how to use it properly, and not end up being used by it. Take a moment to reflect on how much you depend on money in your life. Make it a point that from now on, the influence of money over your life will be very much limited, and that you will never depend on it anymore for happiness.

Quick Review

- What is money in the modern world?

- How important is money to you?

Introspection

The practice of introspection is very important. Introspection is simply self-examination. It is looking within to help understand yourself better. It is very easy to get lost in this world. We must be careful to preserve our own identity and character. It is a highly recommended practice that you form it as a habit to look within yourself every now and then. Examine your life and how you are living it.

A good way to do introspection is by writing down the things that you want to examine about yourself. This will allow you to view yourself from a different perspective, from an angle that is without any bias and prejudice. It will also allow you to think outside the box. You should also pay attention to the thoughts that you often keep and entertain in your mind. Are they good, positive, and happy thoughts?

When you practice introspection, it is important that you become very open and honest with yourself. Many people commit the mistake of focusing only on their strengths and keeping a blind eye on their weaknesses. However, you must know that you will benefit the most when you acknowledge your weaknesses. This will allow you to work on them and even turn them into strength.

Introspection is a time that you spend with yourself. It does not have to be a long time. In fact, even 20 minutes will do. Make it a habit to practice this as often as you can. I know some people who like to do this every night just before going to bed. There are no strict rules on how to get about doing this or how often you just engage in this practice, but be sure to make positive efforts to take advantage of this practice. While you are at it, also spend time to reflect on your current relationship with money. How much influence does money have in your life? Another thing to consider is your desire to earn money, as well as how much money you are desiring. By being open and honest with yourself, the more that you will understand who you really are, as well as how you can better deal with all the financial issues and matters in your life.

Quick Review

- What is introspection?

- How often should you practice introspection?

- Why should you acknowledge your weaknesses?

Necessary Expenses

Let us now talk about the part where money becomes necessary. Indeed, as long as you are exposed to this world, money will be important. No matter how frugal you intend to live, there are parts in our life where we really have to spend money. The only people I know who do not spend any money at all are those who are living offgrid, such as those who isolate themselves in the desert or in a rainforest, among others. However, let us accept the fact that this is simply not that practical and doable for most of us. For many of us, we have no choice but to continue living within the system of the modern world. Hence, being frugal means spending less money, and not the complete renunciation of money.

So, we do have to accept the fact that we will also be needing and spending money regularly. However, this time, we now know that we do not need a huge amount of money, which means that we can have more free time in our hands (for earning more money usually means having to work for more hours). This time, we can focus more on the things that really matter to us, and most especially our family and loved ones.

For this exercise, you will just need a pen and paper. Note down all your current expenses. Be sure to include the actual amount of money that you are spending for these expenses. Now, look at your list and try to see if they are all necessary expenses. It is quite usual to be able to find that some of the things that we are spending money on are not actually essential in our life. If you ever find such unimportant things on the list, cross them down.

The next step is to look for items on the list that you can lower. For example, instead of buying ten packs of cigarettes a month, you can make it just 6 packs per month. Try to look for other similar items that you can still cut down the cost.

Next, try to find ways that you can further cut down the items on the list. You should end up with a list of items that are absolutely essential in your life, both for your survival and comfort. Take note that this is not just about being alive, but your comfort is also considered necessary. After all, frugal living does not mean uncomfortable living. You deserve to be happy and comfortable with your life. It is not an extreme approach to life. It is not asceticism, but it is simply a better way of living your life in a way that is not fully dependent on money.

You do not need to follow the aforesaid steps strictly. The key point here is to have a clear view of your necessary expenses and to try to lower your overall expenses as much as you can. The lower your expenses are, the less money that you will need — and it may also mean a higher saving. Now, the less money that you need, the more time you will have to enjoy life.

There are people who get so surprised after doing the aforementioned exercise. Sometimes it takes some focus before we realize that we have been spending our money on things that we do not actually need. So, just take note of your necessary expenses and try to lower all your expenses as much as possible and as much as comfortable for you.

Quick Review

- What are the recommended steps to analyze and lower your necessary expenses?

- Should you also sacrifice your comfort when you live a frugal life?

Enjoy the Free Stuff

In this modern world, there are many things that you can enjoy for free. If you focus on these free things, you may consider yourself very rich. For example, there are many videos and contents online that you can consume without having to pay anything. Of course, you may have to pay for internet connection, but internet fees are usually fixed and very affordable; nevertheless, you can enjoy so much free stuff online. There are many ebooks, articles, movies, music, and games that you can get your hands on for free. Be sure to take advantage of this.

In the past, we usually had to pay for a new game or to watch a movie; but with the use of modern technology, this is now something that we can easily do and enjoy for free. This is how we take advantage of the modern world. Indeed, the modern world has its many evils, but it also has certain advantages that we can benefit from and even abuse to our liking.

Many people take the free stuff for granted, maybe because many have this perception that free stuff can be easily taken for granted, but this is actually not true. It is good to enjoy free stuff, especially the ones that we can find online. There is so much knowledge and entertainment that we can enjoy with just an internet access.

Free stuff is not limited to the internet and technology. Be sure to also enjoy the beauty of nature, as well as quality time with your family and friends. As the saying goes, the most beautiful things in life are free. Watch the stars in the night, spend quality time with your loved ones, enjoy a free movie in the evening, feel and breathe the fresh air, hug a tree, and so on. There are many things to enjoy and be busy about without having to spend even a dime. Be sure to take advantage of these things. Why spend money on something when you can enjoy something perhaps even greater for free? And, since these things are free, you can say that you are very rich when it comes to these things. Fortunately, these are usually also the things that really matter in life.

Quick Review

- What are the free stuff that you can enjoy?

- Are free stuff worthless?

The Beauty of Simplicity

Being simple is beautiful. The beauty of a flower is never complex. In fact, its beauty lies in its simplicity. Everything in nature is simple, and that's what makes them beautiful. In our modern world, we tend to complicate things, and this usually causes lots of stress and unnecessary pressure. Frugality teaches us to return to being simple, back to our original state. It simplifies our spendings and expenses, our outlook in life, as well as how we handle things.

As you may already realized by now, being frugal means so much more than spending less. But rather, it is a way of life and a way of thinking. It creates a change within us which expresses itself outward through the way we treat money. It is a simple approach that helps one to be simple and beautiful.

Simplicity saves us from all the complications of this life. It allows us to focus and fully experience what is essential, taking away what we do not need. Many times, we are distracted by so many things and stuff that our minds become cluttered. When this happens, it could cloud our judgement and prevent us from seeing things clearly. This is another trap of the modern world that we should be cautious of.

Being simple means a life that is full of meaning where energy is not scattered among so many unnecessary things. This is also something that being frugal teaches where we focus on what is essential and let go of the things that we really do not need.

Simplicity requires sacrifice or an act of letting go. Do not be discouraged because this is actually good for you. In the beginning, you will have to let go of things that you do not need. We usually keep some things in our life only because we have gotten used to it. It is this habit that we have formed which makes it difficult to let go of certain things, even those things that are totally useless to us. But, we must realize that the more we let go and be as simple as we can be, the more that we can experience freedom, peace of mind, and joy. Hence, the act of letting go into simplicity is an act of love that you give to yourself — because you deserve to be free.

A wise artist once said that true art is not about adding, but a matter of subtracting, of removing what is not essential. To achieve simplicity, we also take away what is not important, leaving us only with who we truly are — and this is what being beautiful is about: be you.

True simplicity is not about being poor or cheap. In fact, simplicity shows a refined taste since it allows you to know what it is that you truly want.

Stop for a moment and consider your life. What are the things that you may let go to make your life simple? This may not always be about things. It may also refer to things that you do that may not be necessary or fun anymore. Remember that the more that you let go, the lighter you will be, enabling you to be simple and fly (freedom). Just give it a try and see how it works for you.

Quick Review

- What is simplicity?

- How can you be simple?

- Is simplicity the same as being poor and cheap?

Learn from Nature

Look around you and observe nature as it is. Do you notice just how frugal and simple nature is? And, that actually makes it beautiful. Nature does not spend any money, but it is merely being as it is — and that is what makes it truly beautiful.

Flowers do not keep their beauty from others, neither do they try to be something else. The Sun keeps on shining and does not assume another form or shape that it is not. Everything in nature gives and receives without the use of money, and they continue to live through and through. Nature is simply beautiful in its most sublime sene. The beauty of their simplicity makes them genuine and real.

We, humans, can also learn from nature. By being who we truly are, by being ourself, we can also share in the beautiful simplicity of nature. After all, we are an important part of nature. We are nature, breathing and moving in life — in line with the rhythm of the universe. It is when we step out of this natural rhthym when problems usually occur, such as stress, pressures, depression, and a sense of dread and even horror.

We can learn from nature to let go just as the wind let go of many things so that it could move freely. We can learn from the stars to keep shining, especially in darkness. We can learn from the flowers to be open to love, and to always give love no matter what the circumstances might be. We can learn from the trees that we can take and receive; and in turn, we also give — for sharing unconditionally is the rhythm of life.

We do not always need money. We can do good deeds without payment. Goodness is free; kindness is free, even forgiveness is free. From now on, let us join in the dance of the universal life force and be one with nature. We are nature, but we need to be ourselves to take active part in this beautiful dance of life.

<u>*Quick Review*</u>

- What can we learn from nature?

- Should there always be money involved to do acts of kindness and goodness?

- How can we more actively join in the music of the universe, the dance of life?

What about Work?

For those who are living the frugal lifestyle, work is true joy, and it is very important. These days, so many people are engaged in the line of work that they are personally not interested in. This is actually a sad thing. Many people work for money, not sincere service.

Now that we know that we do not need a huge amount of money to be happy, we are strongly encouraged to pursue the work that we really love. Income should only be secondary. These days, competition is also very fierce. If you are in a field of work that you do not really like, how are you going to compete with those who are truly passionate in what they are doing? Indeed, with some skill and strong will, there is a chance that you can beat the competition. However, just imagine the toll and all the stress and pressure that this will take on you.

Frugal living makes us realize that we are not under the spell and control of money, and that we always have a choice on how we live our life. Our work should be something that drives our passion and makes us feel good. It is this fire of passion that makes living so beautiful. Those who live the frugal lifestyle usually have this fire continuously burning, thereby allowing them to experience life in a positive way.

If our work is something that we truly love, then it will even be a source of joy for us. While other people are stressed out and unhappy with their work, you can enjoy every part of it and feel peaceful. Having this kind of life is a significant advantage over those who are not happy with their work. The good news is that this is something that you can do right now. Make your work your life's calling. Make it special — and you can make it special by pursuing the work that you love.

But what about if you cannot change your work into the one you love because you really need money to support your family? In this case, if your circumstances so warrant, then you can still engage in the same line of work as you are now doing, but just be sure to take good care of your mental health. Being engaged in a work that you do not like is not a joke. It can be depressing, especially in the long run. Try to make it fun and enjoyable as much as you can, and do not forget the reason why you are doing that work to the point that you have sacrificed the work that you really love for it. In the end, it is still the power of love that compels and moves you.

Quick Review

- How can one's work be turned into true joy?

- Should we work just for money?

- What can you do if you really cannot change your job due to your current needs and circumstances?

Frugal Living & Peace of Mind

Living frugally, if done the right way, can significantly help us attain peace of mind. It should be noted that frugal living is based on a foundational knowledge which pertains to your outlook in life. It would be hard, if not impossible, to pursue frugal living simply by spending less without establishing any foundation for it.

Once you know that you are no longer dependent on money, you can start making better choices and real changes in your life. The things that you do may change (this time with more emphasis on people and things that are really important to you), as well as how you make decisions and view life as a whole.

Frugal living does not only declutter our life, but it also declutters our mind, and this is very important especially these days when so many people are bombarded with so many things to worry about. Frugal living helps us realize the things that are truly important, and it teaches us to let go of those things that we do not really need. This can significantly improve one's quality of life.

To live frugally means that you now know what is truly important to you. It means that you have chosen to let go of the things that you do not need so that you can focus on what is essential. It means that you have freed yourself from the many illusions of the world.

Peace of mind is quite hard to attain these days. The modern man has been programmed to be always bombarded with so many things and stresses in life to the point that if you are not stressed enough, then you are probably not doing enough. Or, a demon might even whisper, "You are not important." But, such kind of programming is wrong and even demonic. It was not so in the Old Days, a time when men and women were one with nature and living a happy and peaceful life. Back then, it was much simpler, and people were always happy. Of course, there was also stress brought about by work, but it was very much manageable. But, these days, especially in our present modern time, minds are subject to slavery. There is no wonder why according to official records, every 40 seconds, somebody in this world dies by suicide. There is simply something very wrong going on here, but people do not seem to care. Everyone is continuously playing along with the dance of death.

The world is already masking all its evils and all its sufferings through the use of social media. When we look at online social media, we always see people who are happy and having a blast in their lives. This creates an idea that the world is doing just right; and that if you have a problem, there is just something wrong with you since everyone else is having a good time. You can see them all online having the time of their lives and everything is well, right? Answer: No. In fact, I have met a number of such people. They have wonderful posts online as if they were living the best lives only to find out that they are actually very problematic, even to the point of committing suicide at times.

Having peace of mind is important, and this is something that you can achieve right now, at this very moment. The way of frugal living gives us a chance to create real and positive changes in our lives in a way that is within your power to do. It is just up to you to apply the teachings and make them work in your life. You can do it. After all, you deserve to enjoy peace of mind. The laws and powers of the universe remain the same even though our world has changed. If our ancestors enjoyed peace of mind, you can do it, too. But, you need to take positive actions to create positive changes in your life. Nevertheless, this is well within your power to do, and you can do it.

Quick Review

- How does frugal living help you attain peace of mind?

- Can achieving peace of mind through frugal living still be possible in our modern time?

- Should you believe all the things that you see on social media?

- According to official records, how often is suicide in our world?

When It is Time to Let Go

I am somebody with so many interests. If you are like me, things may be quite challenging, even confusing. Since we are trying to cover all possible bases and situations to help you actually get your start on frugal living, let us now talk about a certain situation where you also have so many interests or hobbies/passions, and you are trying to simplify your life. What should you do?

Indeed, this can be a problem. The good news is that there are no strict rules on this matter. If you think that you are comfortable with keeping all those hobbies and stuff, then do so. However, if you are like me who really wants to simplify things so that we can give enough time and focus on our chosen craft, then what I did is to reflect and finally make a decision to choose: choose which ones you will keep and those that you will let go.

I happen to have so many interests and if I tried to hold on to all of them, I simply would not have enough time to spend time with all of them. So, yes, it was like a sacrifice—but it was actually something good; otherwise, my time and energy would be divided, and I would not end up anywhere that would be desirable for me. So, after some reflection, I realized only to keep the things that I truly love, such as writing, for example. And then, I summoned the courage to let go of the things that I really do not need but would only take away my time and focus from the things that are truly important to me. Although letting go may not be easy, it is doable. After some time, and now looking back, I would say that I am happy with my choices, and that letting go just happened to be an important step. Birds could not fly if you tied them down to so many things that they would have to carry. The lighter they are, the higher that they can fly.

The principle applies to us. We cannot bombard ourselves with so many things to do and worry about. We must choose our path, our craft or art, and then give it all that we have got. It is how we pursue our dream: we go all in.

Quick Review

- What do we do if we have so many interests and hobbies that we are holding on to?

- Why is it good to free ourselves from unnecessary things?

Pursue Your Dream

Those who are living the frugal lifestyle know what is important in their lives. When it comes to what is important, then pursuing your dream is considered very important. When a man is not pursuing or living their dream, the soul will slowly suffocate, and then it will gradually lose all sense of life and beauty to the point that life as a whole loses its meaning. Indeed, we are all called to pursue our dream. So, what is your dream?

Sad to say, but many people today have already forgotten to dream. They have been misdirected and lost in the modern world that they simply do not know their real self anymore. But, do not be disheartened. If you are one of these people who have gotten lost, know that it is not over for you. You can always find yourself and begin again with a fresh start, a clean slate. Much like a writer turns to a new page to start a new chapter or story, you can reinvent your life and begin again.

Let me ask again: what is your dream? Are you truly living your dream? Dreams are not always meant to be achieved in its whole, but they are always meant to be lived. As they say, it is not reaching the top of the mountain that matters but the journey itself.

Once you know that you are pursuing your dream, a sense of enthusiasm, passion, and even life will enter you—and this is something that you will be able to feel. It is like you are young again, where the miracles of life are always at play, and you are an important part of it. Since you are following the frugal living lifestyle, you now know that money is not your main objective or goal in life. If you do this, and if you pursue your dream with the right mindset, then you will see that your life has new meaning, and that it is much more enjoyable to live in, despite the many faults and evils in the world. However, before you can live this kind of life, you must first have the right foundation (which is also what we are doing in this book), know what your dream is, and then pursue it with all that you have got.

But, what is your dream? If you seem confused and or if you feel like you have lost it somewhere along the way, do not be afraid. Just relax and give yourself some time to identify it. Knowing your dream is like choosing from among the many mountains that you can climb. Our dream is often the one where our enthusiasm or passion leads us. It is something that gives excitement to the soul.

There are no hard and fast rules on how we should choose our dream. It is much like choosing a partner in life. It just happens. Your heart simply knows it. However, you must be very careful that in choosing your dream, you must not allow the rotten world to be the one to choose it for you. Do not worry; you do not need to do this in a rush. Take as much time as you can. In fact, you do not even need to be too serious about it. Instead of being too serious, just enjoy the journey and have fun. This is not difficult at all, even very young kids can tell you their dreams in life. Indeed, adults can learn so much from children.

Quick Review

- What is the importance of pursuing your dream?

- What is your dream?

Going Off-Grid

There are those people who fall in love with frugal living and would love to take it to the next step: a life without money. Now, let us be practical about this approach. In our modern world, although it is doable, it is simply not that convenient and comfortable. As long as you are exposed to the modern world, a part of your life will have to depend on it. So, there are people who completely leave the modern world behind by going off-grid. This means going somewhere far from modern society and living on your own. This is much like the Old Days where the environment should be full of nature, unblemished by human technology.

For this purpose, you may have to go to the desert or the rainforest. It is up to you to choose which environment you would like to live in. However, a common problem with this approach is safety. Since we have been raised in a modern environment, we do not know how to properly survive in wild nature. Hence, this book presents a much more convenient and easier way of living, which is being frugal while still living in the modern world. Still, if you want to take it a step much further, then going off-grid would be a choice for you, but just make sure that you are ready for it.

There are people who have made this happen. Indeed, there are people right now who are living off-grid and are very happy with their lives. Many of them even come from highly professional backgrounds. They often have a common theme in their story: they all found the modern world and workplace too intoxicating and felt that their souls wanted to connect more with nature, away from modern society. It is not really about hating people, but the system has just become so corrupt already that it is too intoxicating to be exposed to it. Sad to say, many people have also really turned bad and lost their humanity because they want to please the system. Having said that, even if you ever want to go off-grid, be sure to equip yourself with the knowledge on how to survive in the environment that you will be living in. If you want to avoid this hassle, then just stick to the frugal lifestyle, so that you can enjoy the benefits of the modern world while at the same protecting yourself from the negative impacts of its system. It is also much easier to do. In fact, you can start doing it right now.

<u>*Quick Review*</u>

- What does living off-grid mean?

- Should you live off-grid?

- If you decide to live off the grid, what should you prepare for?

Money Management

Those who live a frugal lifestyle are not really living off the grid. Just the fact that you are frugal in spending money means that you are making use of money, which means that you are living in the world. But, a big difference is that unlike most people who have made money a huge importance in their lives, money is simply not much in your list of priorities in life. Now, we are not saying that this is the right way and the other is the wrong way, or vice versa. But, this is just a matter of personal preference and a choice. It would be useless to enter into an argument into which way of life is better. There are advantages and disadvantages in every option. But, personally, I feel that frugal living is the kind of life that I love and I could be proud of. It is simple and beautiful at the same time. It is also an easy life with so much meaning. Still, it is up to you to make a choice and reinvent your life in any way that you want. You are free—or at least, you are supposed to be free—free and happy.

So, we should be frugal in spending money. We are rich in love and peace, but when it comes to spending money, we ought to be frugal as we might not have so much of that commodity since we are now focused on something else.

When it comes to money management, it helps to write everything down in a notebook. Write down all your spendings and the income that you have. Just make sure that your income is higher than your expenses, which is a basic rule in budgeting your money. It is actually very simple; and since you are living a frugal life, then I would assume that you will not end up with a very long list to compute.

By now, you should have just a simple list to deal with. If you still have a long list of expenses, then perhaps you have to reexamine your life and note down the things that you truly need to exist and be happy. But, if it really happens that you have a long list despite all efforts to make things simple, then perhaps so be it. Just make sure that you do not lose touch of the teachings and the spiritual value of being frugal. Again, we no longer depend on money for happiness. We just see and use money as it should be, and nothing more. We use money, not the other way around. So, do all your best to manage your money properly. I suggest making a list of all of your monthly expenses and then apply whatever income you have. Along the way, do all your best to minimize whatever expenses that you may have—without sacrificing so much of your comfort, of course. After all, being frugal is not a life of suffering, but it means living with meaning and happiness.

Quick Review

- What is a good way to manage your money?

- Should you write down your money-management plan?

- Should your expenses be higher than your income?

A Message

I hope that you have enjoyed reading this book. I, myself, am also living the frugal lifestyle. I have also taken a vow of poverty. It is not a formal thing but just something I made up. If you want, you can do the same. Under this vow, you promise not to depend on money anymore and to enjoy a personal life of poverty. I am not religious, so please do not take the word "poverty" too literally. But, yes, even though I may have money, I keep very little in my wallet—mainly just in case of emergency. I also do not spend a lot on myself. I have just come to love this kind of lifestyle.

My family is not following this kind of life, so all the money goes to them. I do not really care about money; so as far as I am concerned, I am still happy with my personal life being frugal. I am also bad at numbers, so being frugal saves me the hassle of having to deal with so many numbers.

Another advice that I have is to focus on spirituality. This has been my life-long interest and passion, and perhaps it was also what led me to this kind of slow and frugal lifestyle. If you are also into spirituality, then I strongly suggest that you focus on it and go deep into it. It is also good to note that the monks—the real genuine monks—are living proof that one can be very happy and peaceful in life while having very little material possessions.

I would also like to emphasize that being frugal is not really just about spending less money. It is not really how you spend money that is the key here. But, it is one's view in life, as well as the things that you prioritize and consider as very important in your life. Spending less money and not relying on money are just the effects of a certain realization of life. This is the "foundation" that I was referring to in our previous discussion. If we have this foundation, then being frugal will happen naturally for you will no longer want to depend on money for your life, for peace of mind, and for happiness.

Last but not least, enjoy your life and be happy. Your family and all the people who truly love you also want you to be happy, just as you also wish for them to be very happy. Happiness is a choice, and you always deserve it.

About the Author

www.charlzdelacruz.com

Password to enter the private page: ANGEL912

Don't miss out!

Visit the website below and you can sign up to receive emails whenever Gideon Crusader publishes a new book. There's no charge and no obligation.

https://books2read.com/r/B-A-VRRV-KRYCC

BOOKS2READ

Connecting independent readers to independent writers.

Did you love *Frugal Living for Happiness & Freedom*? Then you should read *Create an Alter Ego for Work Success and Peace of Mind*[1] by Charles Mage!

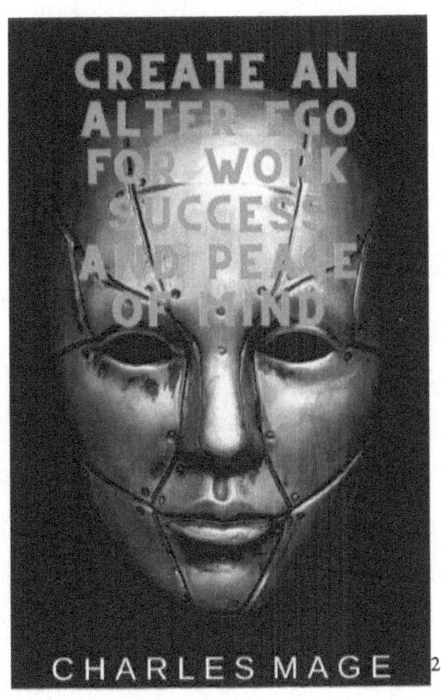

[2]

Create an Alter Ego for Work Success and Peace of Mind is a life manual that teaches the secrets of creating a different persona or your alter ego to handle all the work for you. Are you being bombarded with so much stress and pressures at work? Are you having a hard time dealing with people at work? Have you realized that you cannot be your true self at work? Do you want to be more efficient and effective at work? Does your real personality conflict with the personality that you need for work?

---

1. https://books2read.com/u/bz1QBL

2. https://books2read.com/u/bz1QBL

If you have answered yes to any of these questions, then this book is for you.

Creating an alter ego is a great way to manage stress and all the work that you do. This way, all the negative energies will be handled by your alter ego as your real self remains pure and undefiled by the modern world. Yes, this is something that you can do, and all it takes is a shift in your mindset and the way you view things.

These days, many professionals are sad and unsatisfied with their work. Work has become so stressful and problematic that it is no longer fun. By creating an alter ego, things will be a lot more manageable for you, and you will no longer be directly affected by the stresses and pressures of your work.

Create an Alter Ego for Work Success and Peace of Mind teaches the ins and outs of creating an alter ego that can help you with your work, but you can also apply the same technique to help you with other matters of your life. But, this book is focused on work-related matters. Indeed, by the time that you finish reading this book, you will have the power to create an alter ego that will allow you to live your best life.

I learned about this technique when my life got very stressful. I am a professional who engages directly with people, helping them resolve their problems. After some time, I realized that I was already suffering, and I was suffering really badly. I was earning more money but my level of happiness was almost gone. I became depressed and extremely vulnerable that even my family was already being affected. But, once I learned to create an effective alter ego, I became untouchable to the stresses of work, and I returned back to my true self -- happy and peaceful all the time. This book has been written to help share what I have learned, so that if you are also caught in the same or similar challenges in life, then here is the way out -- a key to power and a way to true happiness and peace of mind.

Read more at https://www.charlzdelacruz.com/.

Also by Gideon Crusader

Magic Quest
A Codex on Creating a Magical Phantom
Prosperity Magic for Money & Wealth
Telekinesis Bible
Beware of the Modern World

Standalone
Frugal Living for Happiness & Freedom

www.ingramcontent.com/pod-product-compliance
Lightning Source LLC
Chambersburg PA
CBHW031427160726
47993CB00003B/1440